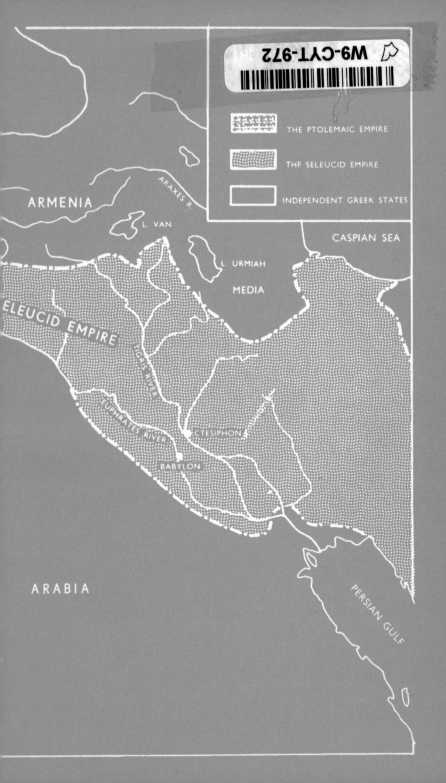

On Your Bar Mitzvah,

For a happy, meaningful life
as a 20th Century American
Jew —

Pearl & Gene Malkis

THE EPIC
OF THE
MACCABEES

by Valerie Mindlin
& Gaalyahu Cornfeld

THE MACMILLAN COMPANY • NEW YORK 1962

THE MACMILLAN COMPANY
NEW YORK
BRETT-MACMILLAN LTD.,
GALT, ONTARIO

Layout and Jacket Design by Paul Kor
PRINTED IN ISRAEL
Peli-P.E.C. Printing Works Ltd.Ramat Gan

Contents

CHAPTER I

PALESTINE IN THE HELLENISTIC WORLD

IN THE WAKE OF ALEXANDER'S CONQUESTS

Outside the tent, the soldiers stood in a long line. They moved slowly and the sun over the Babylon plain was hot. But they waited, silent and sad. Slowly, one by one, they filed into the tent and stood for a moment to bid an unspoken farewell to the man who lay there dying.

The man was Alexander the Great. In eleven years (333-323 B.C.E.) his great conquests had brought Greek culture right across the ancient world from the shores of the Mediterranean to the Indus River in North India.

The Greeks taught that mind and body should be used to the full, that thought could range in all directions, that gymnastics and sports and dancing were part of the life of any healthy man and that every side of life should be made as beautiful as possible. This hellenic culture spread throughout the ancient world, affecting religions, thought, art-forms and the whole tempo of day-to-day living, changing the history of every one of the conquered peoples.

To the ancient peoples of the orient, it opened the door to a brighter, more exciting, happier life. Eagerly they grasped at the new ways, taking the aspects that most appealed to them, changing them to suit different conditions and moulding them to fit into ancient oriental traditions. The resulting mixture of cultures was to be known as "hellenism", its products "hellenistic". Throughout the Near East, this became the predominant fashion.

A SMALL NATION THAT RESISTED HELLENISM

But one people resisted — the Jews. Proudly they clung to the memory of their biblical past. In their remote hills of Judea, hellenism came face to face with deeply rooted Jewish traditions. Inevitably, the two cultures clashed. To the Jews the new ways and above all the new ideas about religion came as something altogether alien to their ancient customs. They, too, might easily have accepted the easier, more prosperous, more attractive way of living, becoming just another minor province within the new hellenistic kingdoms arising in the Near East. Instead, they stood firm against the alien efforts to change them. They did not do so at once, and not always willingly. Many Jews felt strongly attracted to the new life. But others would not yield to foreign influence and foreign domination. They had inherited from their ancestors a faith in one God which no other people shared. They clung tenaciously to the lofty thinking of their prophets and their stern biblical laws.

In the face of overwhelming odds, the Jewish people took up arms against the mighty hellenist power in defence of their own ways and their own religion. Their leader was Judas Maccabaeus. He and his little band of warriors, the "Hassidim" at their head, won national independence for their people and made way for some of the most glorious years in Jewish history. More than this, their fight consolidated Judaism and made possible all the later developments of Jewish and European history. Without their stand, Jewish religion would never have found its way into world history; Christianity would never have arisen in the manner that it did and the whole history of Western European civilization would have been altered.

Our story begins, therefore, at the point where hellenism started the prolonged process which led eventually to civil war in Judea.

THE EMPIRE BREAKS UP

Alexander's armies began by defeating the declining Persian empire which had been for so long an impenetrable barrier between East and West. With this swept away, Alexander dreamed of creating a single unified kingdom from west to

Chariot races in the arena of the Roman "Circus Maximus". Modelled on Greek games, (see p. 15), these were on a much vaster scale. The excitement of the race, among the contestants and their supporters in the galleries, has been vividly captured (see last page for acknowledgments of all illustrations).

east with new hellenistic ways replacing the ancient habits, beliefs and customs of the Eastern peoples.

But in 323 B.C.E. Alexander died. With him died his dreams of empire. None of his generals was strong enough to take his place and instead of one united domain, bitter squabbles between rival leaders finally resulted in the establishment of

three new kingdoms, each with its own Greek king :
Macedonia in Europe, Asia Minor and Syria under
the "Seleucids", and Egypt under the "Ptolemies".

Judea, Samaria and Galilee (later called Palestine) lay between Syria and Egypt, holding the
key to the rich trade with Egypt in textiles, slaves,
wine and foodstuffs. Both the Ptolemies of Egypt
and the Seleucid kings of Syria wanted control of
the area. Four times they fought over the country.
Then, in 301 B.C.E., the Ptolemies finally defeated
the Seleucids and for the next hundred years, Palestine was part of the victorious kingdom.

The Ptolemies ruled Palestine until 200 B.C.E. and, during all this century, life went on peaceably. The country, in those days, was fairly densely populated, its landscape dotted with villages, towns and cities. The Jews lived mainly in the hilly central areas of Judea and Galilee. In the villages, the men were tenant-farmers, craftsmen and labourers, able to read a little, but mostly ignorant. They heard the law of Moses read by a resident priest and interpreted by the scribes and tried to abide by it as closely as they could. One rule they tried to keep was that three times every year, each male Jew from every corner of Palestine and the surrounding countries must visit Jerusalem and offer sacrifice in the Temple. Jerusalem and the Temple were the center of the country's life and great crowds of pilgrims gathered there especially for the festivals of the Passover, and the Feast of Tabernacles (Sukkoth).

The aim of life for the Jews was to live according to the Laws of Moses as laid down and expanded in the scriptures, and embodied in their ancestral customs. For them, there was no aspect of life which was not covered by these rules and, consequently, their High Priest was both their religious leader and their ruler, acting like the kings of other lands.

For instance, it was the High Priest who had to approve the signal given for the beginning of each month. The people had no calendar. A new month began with each new moon. This was eagerly watched for and, as soon as it was seen, the news was rushed to the High Priest's council, the Sanhedrin, in Jerusalem, by men of good character who were closely questioned about their evidence. It was no use if they had merely seen the new moon's reflection in water, or glimpsed it through glass. Then their evidence would be discounted.

Once it had been established that it really was shining, a beacon would be lighted on the top of the Mount of Olives and, from this, a chain of signal fires would be lighted right through the country. A picturesque, if laborious method of knowing one day from another! It was unreliable sometimes, too. The Samaritans were traditionally the enemies of the Jews and sometimes they lighted a misleading beacon on top of their Mount Gerizim, and enjoyed the confusion that resulted!

Around the High Priest in Jerusalem lived the aristocracy of the priesthood and the leaders of secular society; landowners, merchants and wealthy men, with their supporting population of craftsmen, shopkeepers and workers. Their hellenist overlords left the Jews to themselves and life went on peacefully with no apparent threat to Jewish traditions.

In fact the first hint of danger came from among Jews who wanted to abandon the tradition of keeping themselves apart. Alexander had dreamed of spreading Greek culture to all the peoples of the Near East and he had done more than dream. Wherever they went, Alexander and his armies established new towns and settlements. After his death, many of his soldiers did not return to Macedonia, but made new homes for themselves in Palestine, Syria, Egypt and Asia Minor. They married women from the countryside around and built towns, like Samaria in Palestine, which grew into the centers of life for their new homelands.

A hoard of silver coins, (tetradrachmas), left by a Samaritan who fled from Shechem when it was captured by the Seleucids around 200 B.C.E. His name, Simonides, had been scratched on a potsherd (below).

Round towers stood on either side of the entrance to the western gate of Samaria, which was rebuilt by the Greeks on the ruins of the Biblical town.

THE HELLENISTIC APPEAL

The older towns had been untidy, unplanned huddles of houses, crowded for security within a walled enclosure. The new towns, built on Greek models, were spacious and beautiful, with straight colonnaded streets running at right-angles to each other, with stone-built palaces and temples, theatres and baths. As a rule they were named after their founders, like Alexandria in Egypt, the most famous, named after Alexander himself. Acre in Palestine was re-named Ptolemais after Ptolemy.

The cities were organized like a Greek "polis"-Greek for "town", from which comes our word "politics" — town affairs. Every citizen had a vote in the elections for the town's ruling assembly. Later on, the poorer citizens lost this right, but it remained the ideal. In the old cities, people had been little more than the slaves of the ruler of the city. Now they learned to think of themselves as citizens, part of the institution of the city, with rights as well as obligations. These were entirely new ideas in the ancient Near East. No wonder they had such appeal !

CITY LIFE

Even though, in the Palestine countryside, life continued unchanged, in the cities, the simple austere ways which the Old Testament had taught the Jews began to give way to an easier, more attractive life. The Greeks loved beauty, not only in art but in the movements of a well-trained body, the creations of a lively mind. Every Greek city, therefore, had its "gymnasium", a school of physical training and "rhetoric" (which meant literature and art as well as politics). Much more than schools as we know them, the gymnasium became the social center and main place of entertainment for the polis, especially for the young men.

The Jews loved games, but their religion had forbidden exhibitions and displays in the hellenistic fashion. Tradition-loving Jews were deeply offended by the sight of athletes exercising naked, Greek fashion, in the gymnasium, or by the plays and poetry that were read there. Nevertheless, the new-fangled ways spread, to the distress of the pious. The author of the Second Book of Maccabees complained bitterly of the effects of the spread of hellenistic ways :

> "... the priests were no longer earnest about the services of the altar, but disdaining the sanctuary and neglecting the sacrifices, they hurried to take part in the unlawful exercises in the wrestling school, after the summons to the discus-throwing, regarding as worthless the things their forefathers valued, and thinking Greek standards the finest." (2 Maccabees 4:14-15)

Even more disquieting was the threat which the hellenistic cities offered to the Jews' religion. According to the Greek model, each city had its own patron god, or goddess, who must be suitably honoured and worshipped. The Jews worshipped one God and could have "no other gods but him". Every step towards greater hellenization seemed to the pious to be flouting this commandment.

THE KING'S TAX-FARMER WAS RICH

For as the new ways gained greater hold many other ancient customs were affected. Administration of Palestine by the Ptolemies meant that the High Priest, as "leader of the people" was also the king's "tax-farmer". In every province of the empire there was a tax-farmer who paid the king a fixed sum of money for royal approval of his high position. Then he appointed his own tax-collectors to get as much money out of the people as possible.

Graceful Greek athlete (compare with pp. 4 and 35).

Jewellery of a third century Syrian nobleman. Above, jewelled gold bracelet. Below, gold arm bands.

It was always far more than the sum he paid to the king. The High Priests, according to the ancient historian, Josephus, paid out at first as much as twenty talents "out of their own estates" for such royal approval. (The heavy silver talent was approximately 60 lbs. of silver, worth about 2,000 dollars, so 20 talents was about 40 thousand dollars, quite a lot of money for those days !).

However, after the Ptolemies had been masters of Palestine for about 70 years, the position changed. The High Priest became an exclusively religious figure, and administration and tax collecting were taken over by a prominent layman. Every year, rich men bid against each other to purchase the post. The one who was prepared to pay most, or who had the most influence, became the king's tax farmer. Each year, a different man could grow rich out of farming the taxes of the land. Soon there was a new class of rich men in Jerusalem, who welcomed every aspect of hellenism.

They built up great fortunes by draining heavy taxes from the farmers in the countryside and the workers in the towns. The old Law of Moses had taught that a rich man had a duty towards the poorer people who served him. These new rich men cared little for that law. They followed the fashionable new ways of their hellenist masters and formed a party to make all Jewry do likewise, that is, to "hellenize" the country. Meanwhile their agents went through the land, arousing universal hatred — and collecting the money.

Among the Jewish ruling classes who adopted the hellenist ways was the Tobiah family, from which came successive "leaders of the people". The best known of these was Joseph-ben-Tobiah. From being "leader" of his own people, he managed to persuade Ptolemy II to appoint him Royal Agent for the whole of Palestine and Coele-Syria (north of Palestine).

The details of Joseph's life and dealings were learned partly from the account given by Josephus and also from a set of ancient archives known as the Zenon Papyri. Zenon was a diligent and dexterous agent of Ptolemy's finance minister, Apollonius. One of his files, containing letters written on papyrus from, to, and about his master, was discovered in Egypt in 1915, twenty two centuries later.

One of the letters, with a date which corresponds to May 12, 259 B.C.E. and written in Greek, was from Joseph-ben-Tobiah to King Ptolemy Philadelphus himself, announcing a present of some wild animals for his majesty's private zoo. The king's zoological garden in Alexandria was famous and pictures of wild animals which have been found elsewhere may have been based on sketches made there. For instance, Joseph's letter speaks of a foal bred from a wild ass. Just such an animal has been found in a painted frescoe on the wall of a tomb in Maresha in Palestine.

This wild ass killing a snake (right) and lynx (left) were part of the elaborate paintings on the walls of the tombs of Maresha in southern Judea.

Joseph had a son, called Hyrcanus, whose life became the basis for many legends, but who was probably a good example of a general trend among the rich men of his time.

Sent on a mission to Alexandria on behalf of Joseph, Hyrcanus managed to get his father's position for himself. Returning, he even tried to take over Jerusalem by force, but was defeated. He fled across the Jordan to the "Land of Tobiah" and there built himself a "strong fortress" from which he went out on raiding parties against the neighbouring Arab tribes.

Long after his death, archaeologists in Palestine found the rock-cut tomb of the Tobiah family at Araq-el-Emir, with the word "Tobiah" in Hebrew-Aramaic letters carved on it like a name-plate.

The name "Tobiah" in Hebrew letters, clearly carved on the mountain rock at the entrance to ancient caverns near the palace of the Tobiads. The upper part of the house, "Beith-Tobia", was decorated by a carved frieze of lions (below). Beneath this, the wall was of huge polished stones while the entrance to the house was between Corinthian-Persian style Greek columns.

Hyrcanus was probably typical of the younger wealthy men who coveted the luxury and intellectual excitement of the hellenist way of life. At the very least, they had their careers to consider. Advancement in any position depended on the favour, or at least the agreement, of the hellenist rulers, but a Jew who stuck rigidly to the strict demands of the Jewish faith was automatically excluded from their circles. To obtain entry he had to relax his standards. Josephus dwells on the iniquity of Joseph-ben-Tobiah eating Egyptian foods at the royal table in Alexandria. There must have been many other examples of the law and customs of Judaism being flouted.

The trend even affected the priesthood. The Temple treasury served as the deposit bank for many of the families and business men of the city and the new ways were good for business. As priest and merchant came together for financial transactions, so the freer thought of the laymen must have had its influence on the religious leaders, whose wealth was also growing.

One effect of this was to emphasize the differences between the priestly aristocracy in Jerusalem, and the humble provincial priests who remained close to the ordinary people, sharing their problems and concerns. The wealthy priests of Jerusalem were remote from ordinary life and neglected the "interpreting" of the Torah, that is, the application of its general rules to the details of actual, everyday problems. This became the task of the Scribes, a class of learned men. The life of the people presented all sorts of questions of behaviour and law. The Scribe would take an appropriate passage from the Bible and expand it into a ruling that answered the problem. These rulings grew into a code of civil laws, known as the Oral Law (because it was handed down orally, not written), which applied the Mosaic Law to daily life. As time went on, the Scribes became the intellectual leaders of the people, whom they understood so well. Later on, a more pious section of the people formed themselves into the groups of Hassidim — devout ascetics, who, from their total, selfless dedication to the Law and the observance of the Priestly Code of Judaism, developed into warrior saints who became the corps d'elite of the Maccabean resistance.

Youths in the wrestling place ('palaestra'), painted on a 2,500 year-old Greek drinking cup.

CHAPTER II

ANTIOCHUS PERSECUTES THE JEWS

PALESTINE'S NEW HELLENISTIC RULERS

After a hundred years of slow development within a Palestine ruled by Egypt, everything was to change. In the year 200 B.C.E., a great battle was fought between the hellenistic kings of Egypt and Syria at a place called Paneion in the north of Palestine. The rulers of Egypt were defeated and lost their control of Palestine. The country became part of the Seleucid empire of Syria and Mesopotamia. The future of Jewry rested with the Seleucid monarchs Antiochus III and his successor, Antiochus IV.

At first the new ruler promised the Jews permission to "live according to their ancestral law" and accepted the self-government of Palestine by the High Priest and his assistants.

But to the hellenizers of Judea, the change-over came as an encouragement. They began plotting to get one of their supporters appointed High Priest. The situation looked so favourable for them, that it aroused the opposition of all those Jews, among the upper class as well as the poorer people, who did not want change, and resented and resisted the attempts of the hellenizers. The very fact that hallowed customs were in danger inspired a movement in their defence. The Jews were proud of their traditions and determined to uphold them. A new wave of nationalism swept through the people of Palestine just as a crisis within the Seleucid empire brought about a changed attitude towards the Jews.

THE SELEUCIDS CHECKED BY ROME

The Seleucid empire which seemed so strong, suddenly came face to face with the rising power of Rome. The Seleucids had been having everything their own way, their armies able to defeat the badly organized forces of most of the native peoples they attacked. Now, Rome was developing the excellently organized and trained soldiers who were taking the Roman eagles further and further afield, intent on inheriting the might and wealth of the empire Alexander had bequeathed to his successors. When one such Roman army clashed with Antiochus' troops in Egypt, they were quickly victorious and demanded a heavy reparations payment from Antiochus.

Just as Antiochus III was desperately looking for a new source of funds to meet this demand, his governor of the province of Coele-Syria (which included Palestine) brought him word that the Temple in Jerusalem was full of treasure, (a fact which had been disclosed to him by Simon, a disgruntled Temple official who was intriguing for high office and hated the High Priest, Onias III).

5th century B.C.E. vases ; (left) a trainer in the 'palaestra' (right) young Judean.

The king sent his chancellor, Heliodorus, to collect. The Second Book of Maccabees tells in detail a lively legend of how Heliodorus' attempts to rob the Treasury were foiled by a "miracle":

> "But no sooner had he and his guards arrived before the treasury than the Sovereign of spirits and of all authority caused a great manifestation so that all who had been daring enough to come with him were appalled at the power of God and fainted with terror. For there appeared to them a horse with a dreadful rider, adorned with magnificent trappings, and rushing swiftly at Heliodorus it struck at him with its forefeet. His rider seemed clad in golden armor. Two young men also appeared to him, remarkably strong and gloriously beautiful and splendidly dressed, who stood on each side of him and flogged him continually, inflicting many stripes on him. He fell suddenly to the ground and was enveloped in deep darkness, and men picked him up and put him on a stretcher and carried him off — the man that had just entered that treasury with a great retinue and his whole guard but was now rendered helpless — and they clearly recognized the sovereign power of God." (2 Maccabees 3:24-28)

The book tells earlier that the threat to rob the Treasury had aroused "no small distress throughout the whole city". It seems reasonable for us to interpret this "miracle" as meaning that Heliodorus was defeated by the united opposition of the High Priest Onias and the people, acting together.

ANTIOCHUS IV AND THE HIGH PRIESTS

However, the High Priest's resistance did not go unpunished. Antiochus IV had been newly crowned in Antioch and he summoned Onias to appear before him to answer charges of plotting against him with the Ptolemies and Hyrcanus, still brooding in the Land of Tobiah. The charges were never proved, but Onias was imprisoned in Antioch and, later, put to death.

Onias was succeeded as High Priest by his brother, Jesus (Yeshua), Jason. The new High Priest agreed to co-operate with Antiochus in his ambition to hellenize Jewry. Antiochus liked to picture himself as the "saviour" of the ignorant natives of his kingdom. He was an impulsive, eccentric monarch who was always trying to do something extraordinary that would make a mark in the world. He chose for himself the title of Epiphanes, "god manifest" (for Greek dynasts were deified). He liked to mix with his people and the Greek historian, Polybius, tells that he used to walk through the streets of Antioch, wearing magnificent robes and crowned with roses, distributing rings of gold or... handfuls of stones to everyone he met.

He determined to bring Greek civilization to all his oriental subjects. He helped the Greek settlements in his dominions and encouraged the setting up of more Greek-style cities.

THE HELLENIZING PROGRAM

Up to this point, the hellenizing program in Judea had not really been an attack on religion. What the hellenizers wanted was that the Jews should abandon their ancient tradition of keeping themselves apart from other peoples and their customs. They said :

> "Let us go and make a treaty with the heathen around us, for ever since the time we became separated from them, many misfortunes have overtaken us." (1 Maccabees 1:11-12).

However, the majority of the people were much more concerned with the misfortunes they feared would follow such a change. Their resentment against the unpriestlike actions of the High Priests grew sharper when Jason was replaced by a son of a Temple official, Menelaus, who was not even a member of the ancient Zadok family of High Priests, and who raided the Temple treasures to send money to Antiochus. His payment to the king was 300 talents (over half a million dollars) more than the sum Jason had paid. Opposition to him led to fighting in the streets of Jerusalem. When rumours spread in Judea that Antiochus had been killed in battle in Egypt, the hellenizers' opponents took what they thought was their opportunity for revenge and set upon the hellenizers. Menelaus escaped with his life but a number of his followers were slaughtered.

ANTIOCHUS MAKES UP HIS MIND

Antiochus had not been killed, but he had been defeated. He had set out on a campaign against Egypt and had laid siege to Alexandria confident of being the victor. But, once again, he was up against more than the Ptolemies. Egypt's rulers

Roman centurion and standard bearer; symbols of Roman might.

had the support of the Roman Senate and Roman legions. The Senate's delegate brought Antiochus a demand to leave Egypt immediately :

"Let me think," said Antiochus to the Senate's messenger, Popilius Laenas.

The Roman drew a circle round the king with his stick,

"Think here."

Antiochus had no choice.

"I shall do as the Senate wishes."

He had to evacuate Egypt and return home.

This defeat made a deep impression on the Syrian ruler. He saw that he had to find some way to fortify his empire against the military strength of Rome and its growing influence in the Near East. He needed to have a united people in his declining empire. To get this, he made up his mind that all his vassal states must be hellenized without exception and without delay.

Above all, it seemed to Antiochus, he must destroy the independent ideas of the little Jewish commonwealth that lay so invitingly on the borders of his rival empire. The Jews of Judea, Samaria and Galilee must learn to obey their king and to worship him and his gods instead of the God they recognized as the single, universal God. Altars to the Syrian-hellenistic gods must be set up in every town and village and the Jews must make sacrifice to them of whatever "unclean" animal might be decreed. Above all, circumcision, the practice that marked them as Jews, must be stopped. The Sab-

Sacrificing a pig to pagan gods. The Syrians even made such sacrifices in the Temple. To the Jews this was "the abomination that makes desolate" (see p. 38). The painting comes from a Greek ceramic platter.

bath must no longer be kept as a day of rest and the great Jewish festivals must go unmarked.

The hellenizing party had already come to blows with the people over this issue. When the fleeing High Priest Menelaus reached Antioch with tales of plots against the Seleucids and civil war in Jerusalem and the rest of Judea, Antiochus made up his mind to crush any attempts at rebellion right at the beginning.

At the head of a strong army he marched into Judea, stormed Jerusalem and "took the city by force of arms". Once in control, with many of the city's defenders lying dead, he despoiled the Temple,

> "... he dared to go into the most holy temple in all the world... and took the sacred plate in his polluted hands and with his profane hands he swept away what had been dedicated by other kings to enhance the glory and honour of the place." (2 Maccabees 5:15-16)

The golden altar, the sacred vessels and all the treasures that had been deposited in the Temple for safe-keeping were carried away. This time there was no miracle. Antiochus returned to Syria, leaving a foreign garrison behind in the Jerusalem fortress.

The Syrian soldiers did not quell the rebellion but, rather, made matters worse. They were pagans who worshipped idols, which to the Jews were merely senseless pieces of stone or metal, made with men's hands. The Jews' God was a being too wonderful and holy for man even to imagine him. It was strictly forbidden to make "any graven image" of God and this rule had always been kept. In all the excavations that have been made of Jewish settlements in Palestine, no single picture, or statue, or carving of their God has been found. They truly worshipped the spirit of God — not his image or picture. When pagan sacrifices were made by the Syrians in the Temple of Jerusalem, it was a desecration that could not be overlooked:

GLADSTONE.

> "Her (Jerusalem's) sanctuary was laid waste like a wilderness, her feasts were turned into mourning, her sabbaths into reproach, her honour into contempt."

laments the First Book of Maccabees (1:39) which takes up the story at this point.

DISTURBANCES IN JERUSALEM

In Syria, Antiochus called for reports on the situation in the southern province. The answers were disappointing. The people of Jerusalem remained almost in a state of war with the hellenizers and there were continual disturbances. Bands of armed men belonging to the ruling party would attack citizens who continued to observe the old customs, or who, perhaps, were being more than usually slow to pay their taxes. And the citizens in turn, of course, retaliated.

Antiochus realized that one action in Jerusalem had not crushed the opposition of a whole country. He asked what was making this insignificant people in its remote and hilly land so unwilling to accept the benefits he was offering. Back came the answer :

"The strength of their religion".

THE BRUTAL PERSECUTION

So, thought the king, this religion must be wiped out. This is how the First Book of Maccabees records the action he took :

Coin of Antiochus IV Epiphanes, the Jews' great enemy and persecutor.

"And the king sent word by messengers to Jerusalem and the towns of Judah to follow practices foreign to the country and put a stop to whole burnt offerings and sacrifices and drink offerings at the sanctuary, and to break the sabbaths and profane the feasts and pollute sanctuary and sanctified; and to leave their sons uncircumcised and defile themselves with every unclean and profane practice so that they might forget the Law and change all their religious ordinances; and anyone who did not obey the command of the king should die." (1 Maccabees 1:44-50).

Thus the king hoped to unite all his empire and be strong enough to have no fears of Rome. But the very brutality of the persecutions defeated his object. Faced by this fierce attack from the foreign power who occupied their country, the people determined to defend their own religion and their traditional ways against all the might of the Syrian empire.

The Syrian soldiers went through the country throwing down the altars, burning the sacred books of the law, killing circumcised babies and their mothers and forcing Jews to sacrifice pigs to pagan gods and — as part of the sacrificial ritual — that meant eating the meat as well. At this,

"... many in Israel stood firm and resolved in their hearts not to eat what was unclean; they preferred death to being polluted with food or profaning the sacred agreement." (1 Mac. 1:62-63)

List of pagan priests in the hellenistic city of Scythopolis (Beath-shean) during the Seleucid period. The Maccabeans never conquered the city and its people went out on raids against their Jewish neighbours.

The Jews were faced with the choice between apostasy (leaving their religion) and rebellion. They chose to rebel. But the rebellion was still unorganized and needed leaders. These came from an alliance between groups of Hassidim and an obscure priestly family of Modiin.

A victorious Greek soldier, tying up his enemy; painted on a 3rd century B.C.E. hellenistic vase. Battles were largely a question of hand-to-hand combat; see the war scenes on pp. 48–49.

CHAPTER III

THE WAR OF LIBERATION

THE BEGINNING OF THE HOLY WAR

"In those days, rose up Mattathias, the son of John, the son of Simeon, a priest of the descendants of Joarib, removed from Jerusalem and settled in Modiin." (1 Maccabees 2:1)

Modiin was a little village about a mile north of the ancient road that ran from Jerusalem to Lod. This was somewhere about 166 B.C.E., thirty years after the first attempt on the Temple by Heliodorus.

Antiochus' edict was probably applied first in the capital where the party of the hellenizers, however much it might be hated, was in power. Indeed on the 15th Kislev (December), a pagan altar — a "dreadful desecration" — was erected in the holy Temple of Jerusalem above the high altar itself.

Thus the hardening of resistance came, not from the official leaders in Jerusalem, but from among the people of the countryside. There, the process of hellenization had hardly begun. The majority of the people held loyally to their ancestral faith and customs. They met the persecution with courage and determined to resist the new regulations.

Among the first to fight back were the Hassidim who could count on the support of the majority of the people of the countryside, and the lower ranks of the rural priesthood. One of these was Mattathias, of the Hasmonean family. Mattathias and his five sons, in the little town of Modiin, "mourned exceedingly" to learn about the persecutions.

Most of our information about the war comes from the First book of Maccabees, the more popular among the ancient books called by that name. Sometimes the evidence of the Second Book is useful for more information about the background to the fighting.

One tradition of the Second Book of Maccabees tells that when the persecutions had reached their peak, Judas fled from Jerusalem with nine other men and hid in the "wilderness". They were joined by bands of Hassidim warrior-saints and by hundreds of patriots. As the avalanche of persecutions rolled on, they filtered back into the villages of Judea and gathered some 6,000 men under the banner of Judas, the Maccabee. Historians are inclined to believe this account.

The narrative of the First Book of Maccabees begins more modestly.

One day, the king's officers came to Modiin to enforce his new regulations. Mattathias' views were known to his neighbours and a crowd gathered to hear how he answered the soldiers' invitation to take the lead in obeying the king.

Declared Mattathias :

"If all the heathen in the king's dominions listen to him and forsake each of them the religion of his forefathers, and choose to follow his commands instead, yet I and my sons and my brothers will live in accordance with the agreement of our fore-

fathers. God forbid that we should abandon the Law and the ordinances. We will not listen to the message of the king, or depart from our religion to the right hand or the left."
(1 Maccabees 2:19-22).

The soldiers had promised him the rich reward of the king's favour if he would do as he was told. Mattathias had refused, but another Jew was ready to take his place. He went up to the altar that had been put up and began to make the pagan sacrifice. Mattathias watched him, his anger growing every moment. And his decision was made. Running forward, he snatched the knife and with it killed the man on top of his sacrifice. Then he turned, killed the officer and pulled down the altar.

This meant open war, and he knew it. Turning to the crowd, Mattathias called: "All who are zealous for the law and the covenant, follow me !"

Then he and his sons fled into the mountains and set up secret centers of resistance. And men joined them. Men whose faith in God had never wavered and who welcomed a chance to strike a blow in His name. Men who had been oppressed, insulted, affronted. Labourers who left their homes in the towns. Farmers who left their lands. All who "sought after justice and judgment" took up arms and prepared to fight.

THE FIRST MARTYRS

One such company, made up of whole families, men with their wives and children and belongings, went into the traditional refuge, the "wilderness"

Two ancient faiths are symbolized by these two objects.
The symbols of Israel's belief
are (left) the eight-branched
Menorah in the upper-left
section of this stone door and,
bottom left, the Ark of the
Scrolls of the Law (the Torah).
Pagan religions are symbolized
(right) by this stone image
of Jupiter-Heliopolitanus, the
Hellenized form of the ancient
Canaanite god, Baal.

of the bare hills south east of Jerusalem. There the Syrian Seleucid forces sent to crush the revolt found them, drew themselves up into battle formation and called on the Jews :

"Either accept the king's laws, or fight !"

But the Jews would do neither. The day was a Saturday, and one of the causes they stood for was observance of the Sabbath. Rather than strike a blow in their own defence and profane the commandment that forbade all activity during that one weekly day of rest, they allowed themselves to be slaughtered to a man.

They were some of the earliest religious martyrs. But obviously, the law had to be changed to meet such emergencies. Mattathias and his friends declared that, in a holy war, fighting was lawful even on the Sabbath and that rule has been followed in Israel ever since.

MATTATHIAS DIES BUT THE STRUGGLE CONTINUES

Mattathias was an old man. A year later he died. Sadly his sons and followers buried him "with his fathers" in the family cemetary in Modiin.

There was no question of giving up the struggle. The partisan army spread through the land, gathering recruits, destroying foreign altars, circumcising male children and taking a heavy toll of the army of occupation. They were led by the Hassidim under the standard of the five sons of Mattathias : the eldest, Johanan, also called Gaddi; Simon called Thassi, reputed the wisest and most prudent; Judas Maccabaeus, "the hammerer", the boldest and most skilful in war who had been the leader from the beginning; Eleazar, the fourth son, called Avaran, and Jonathan, the youngest, with the nickname of Apphus, or "the wary".

THE CHALLENGE OF JUDAS MACCABAEUS

Judas was an inspiring leader and a good general. His very first battle against the local Syrian forces was a splendid victory. Even the Syrian commander of the Samarian province, Apollonius, was killed. Judas took his sword and fought with it "all the rest of his days".

A higher Syrian commander, Seron, governor of the province of Coele-Syria, was sent with a "mighty army". Down the plain of Sharon they marched on the road that ran from Lydda to Jerusalem, passing close to Judas' home of Modiin. Then the great army began the steep ascent of Beth-horon. Nearby was the little village of Ayalon where once Joshua had stood and commanded the sun to stand still until Israel defeated its enemies.

When Judas' men saw the great number of soldiers coming up against them, they were frightened for a moment: "How can we, few as we are, fight with such a strong host?" — they asked Judas worriedly. But Judas was unafraid. He put his trust in God and, "with Heaven it is all one, to save by many or by few."

A dying soldier, sword still in his hand. From a 5th century B.C.E. Greek gravestone

The Syrians were invading a strange land, to which they had no right: "we are fighting for our lives and our laws."

And at Beth-horon, in the hills overlooking the coastal plain, Judas launched a surprise attack. In spite of their much greater numbers the Syrians (hellenists) were routed. They fled, hampered by the unfamiliar country and their equipment.

These victories made Judas famous on both sides of the Jordan and beyond. More and more men came to join him and together they formed the beginnings of a properly organized, well-disciplined army.

Weapons most used by the infantry were the short sword and the lance, shown in this war scene from an Etruscan urn.

They heard of him in Syria too. Antiochus had gone away on a campaign in his eastern empire and he had left his throne and the conduct of affairs "from the River Euphrates unto the borders of Egypt" in charge of his general, Lysias. This included the job of putting down the rebellion in Judea. To head the campaign for the destruction of this unruly people, he chose Nicanor and Gorgias. They led a strong army into Judea and set up camp at Emmaus, where they were joined by more soldiers from Syria and auxiliaries from the hellenist cities and the land of the Philistines who hoped to join in the plunder of Judea.

Gorgias planned to make a surprise attack on the Jewish army and he set out at the head of five thousand of his foot soldiers and a thousand of his best horsemen to take the Jewish camp by night. But Judas had the better intelligence service. As soon as he heard the plan, he took his army out of their camp and, while the Syrians were searching vainly for his men, he suddenly appeared before the Syrian camp and destroyed it. The Syrian army had been marching all night through the mountains, getting lost and finding nothing. When they turned back, they saw their own camp in flames and the Jewish forces waiting for them in the plain in front of it. The Syrians turned and fled. Judas was left with another great victory and, in addition, the rich spoils and stores from the Syrian camp.

Up to this time, Judas had faced mainly the local Syrian forces. Resistance to the Seleucid empire seemed terribly important to the Jews who were actually concerned, but Judea was a very small province of the great hellenist dominions. Difficulties there were still a matter for the local officials.

Now, however, the Syrian governor of Jerusalem, Philip, called upon the provincial governor of Coele-Syria and Phoenicia for help to put down the rebellion, for he saw that Judas was "gaining ground little by little". In fact his victories at Beth-horon and Emmaus had swelled his army to 10,000 men.

Against them, a great army was sent, made up of mercenaries from hellenized Syria and Mesopotamia and the Greek provinces of Asia Minor. The actual numbers were probably much smaller than the ancient documents would like us to believe, although they were certainly better equipped and armed for hand-to-hand fighting and for siege warfare. Judas' forces were heavily outnumbered in most of their battles. But they were fighting a holy war in defence of their religion and their homes. Their spirit was worth an extra battering ram any day !

Judas' army, it seems, consisted of a central mobile body of trained fighters, who were joined in the different parts of the countryside by local bands of partisans. They were usually peasants who left their farms when they were called and went back to the soil when the fighting was over.

From the Second Book of Maccabees, it seems that at about this time, the Jerusalem authorities, the "elders" of the city, who supported the Syrian side in the struggle, decided to try a new tactic. Much of the popularity which Judas' fighters had aroused among the people came from the fact that they were defending the ancient faith. If the persecution of the Jewish religion could be stopped, then he would lose this appeal and his movement would collapse — or so his enemies hoped. The Jerusalem "elders" sent Menelaus to Antioch to request that the "evil decrees" on which the persecution was based be annulled. Two other messengers were sent to General Lysias with a similar plea, and another mission went to ask the Roman Senate to intercede with the Seleucid government in Syria on behalf of the Jews.

Menelaus was successful. He got Antiochus to agree to something that, at first, sounded like a fair offer, although it contained a hidden ultimatum. Antiochus wrote a proclamation to the Jews offering religious freedom and an amnesty to the rebels provided they returned home within fifteen days. But he gave no guarantee that he would keep his side of the bargain.

The hellenizing elders of Jerusalem thought this was a very neat piece of diplomacy. But it didn't succeed in getting rid of Judas. The Syrian forces were withdrawn to meet a more urgent crisis in

The thoughtful face of a 3rd century hellenist.

Fragment of the Scroll of the "War of the Sons of Light against the Sons of Darkness", which may have referred to the wars of the Hasmoneans. It is one of the most important of the Scrolls found in a Dead Sea cave at Qumran.

the east of the empire and Judas made good use of his opportunity.

Six months after he had rejected the offer of the royal proclamation, Judas and his men appeared before the gates of Jerusalem and captured the city. When the Maccabees entered Jerusalem, they were horrified at what they found :

"... the sanctuary desolated and the altar polluted and the doors burned up, and weeds growing in the courts as they do in a wood or on some mountain, and the priests' quarters torn down."
(1 Maccabees 4:38)

Before anything else, this had to be put right and the holy places cleansed.

Judas shut up the Syrian garrison in the Akra — the fortress and garrison of Jerusalem which overlooked the Temple area and the lower town, and controlled them. Then he set out to purify the desecrated Temple and restore it for worship.

The work of restoring the sacred shrine was a task of holy devotion. The First book of Maccabees describes what was done simply, but in a spirit of great joy:

"And Judas appointed priests that were without blemish and adherents of the Law, and they purified the sanctuary and carried out the stones that had defiled it to an unclean place."
(1 Maccabees 4:42-43)
"And they took whole stones as the Law required, and built a new altar like the former one. And they built the sanctuary and the

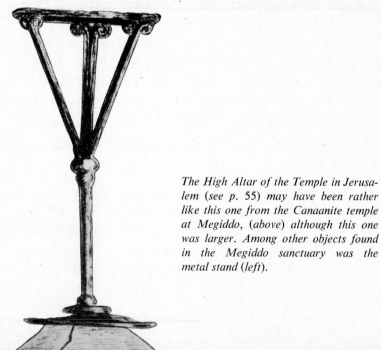

The High Altar of the Temple in Jerusa-
lem (see p. 55) may have been rather
like this one from the Canaanite temple
at Megiddo, (above) although this one
was larger. Among other objects found
in the Megiddo sanctuary was the
metal stand (left).

The Temple once stood on the site of the Dome of the Rock (below) in the middle of this ancient area of Jerusalem. Above, the Jewish Menorah, carved on an ancient lead coffin found in the Beth-Shearim catacombs.

interior of the temple and consecrated the courts. And they made new holy dishes and they brought the lampstand and the altar of incense and the table into the temple. And they burned incense on the altar, and lighted the lamps on the lampstand, and they lighted the temple." (1 Maccabees 4:47-57)

In December 164, three years to the month after its profanation, the Temple was rededicated and the daily sacrifice offered again on the altar. To protect the Temple from enemy attack, a wall was built around Mount Zion where the Temple stood.

"And there was exceeding great gladness among the people and the reproach of the Gentiles was turned away. And Judas and his brethren and the whole congregation of Israel ordained that the days of the dedication of the altar should be kept in their seasons from year to year by the space of eight days, from the five and twentieth days of the month Chislev, with gladness and joy." (1 Maccabees 4:58-59)

This Maccabean edict of Hanukah was never forgotten and the feast of Hanukah has been kept ever since.

HANUKAH, SYMBOL OF THE VICTORY OF THE WEAK OVER THE STRONG

A tradition has been handed down that when the Maccabees regained the Temple, they found nothing undefiled within the sacred precincts except for a small cruse of oil, enough for only one day's lights. Miraculously, however, the lamps filled with the oil continued to burn for eight days. This is the origin of the ancient hymn which is sung today on Hanukah.

From this story has come the sign of the eight daily lights of Hanukah which has ever since represented the Maccabean revolt. A legendary miracle is in any case a fitting symbol for this successful rebellion which seemed so much a miracle itself. The Maccabeans were guerrilla bands protecting a nation which seemed insignificant compared to the might of the great Seleucid empire and the wealth and power of its kings. Yet from the Maccabean movement of national and religious resistance full independence for the Jewish state was to come within the lifetime of the first generation of Hasmonean leaders.

Oil or wine jar from Gibeon (7th century B.C.E.). The Temple's "cruse of oil" may have looked like this.

CHAPTER IV

CONSOLIDATION

Having restored the Temple, Judas drove out the hellenizers and, for a time, Jerusalem was safe from her enemies. But the Jews who lived east of the Jordan in Gilead, or were scattered through Galilee, isolated among strange peoples, were in danger of reprisals.

We are apt to think of the "gentiles" who surrounded the Jews as people living outside Palestine, but, in fact, a large proportion of the people actually living inside the country were not Jewish. The Jewish areas of settlement were separated by the large number of the Greek "poleis" (cities) that dotted Samaria, the coastal region, the Jordan Valley, the South and Transjordan. Many of the gentile towns were hostile to the Jews and were helping the Syrian forces against the Jews. Judas called a council of war to decide what could be done to help their brethren.

He divided his force into three. Three thousand men were sent into Galilee with his brother, Simon, at their head, while Judas and Jonathan, another brother, led eight thousand into Gilead.

RESCUE OPERATION IN GILEAD AND GALILEE

All the Jews were to be rescued. Up to this moment, Judas had been a rebel general. With the capture of Jerusalem he had become a national leader. Although his forces were not strong enough to conquer new territory, they were able to hold the frontiers of the country. If he could bring in the Jews from outside, he could protect them.

In Gilead, Judas established friendly relations with the Nabateans who lived there. Then he faced a series of battles with the occupying Syrians. His fame spread through the country and when the Syrians heard who it was who was leading the army that had invaded Gilead, they were afraid.

Their local general was a man named Timotheus. His army was drawn up at a place called Raphon, on one side of a stream. The general told his captains that the mighty Judas was approaching and if his army crossed the brook and attacked first, they would win. "But," said Timotheus, "if he be afraid and encamp beyond the river, we will cross to him and prevail against him." (1 Maccabees 5:41).

They stood watching the Jewish army as it marched towards the river. At the side of the river, they halted. Judas called the scribes of the army to give them orders — and the hopes of the watching Syrians rose. But the orders were to stand by the edge of the water and "suffer no man to encamp but let all come to the battle." They splashed across the river with swords drawn and, very soon, the Syrians were flinging down their arms and running for cover to the nearby pagan temple at Karnaim. It was soon taken and the temple burned. Timotheus had been utterly defeated.

The victory made it possible for Judas to gather all the Jews of Gilead together and bring them, men, women and children "like a great army" into Judea where they settled in the great plain of Beth-Shean (called Scythopolis by the hellenists),

> "and they went up to Mount Zion with gladness and joy, and offered whole burnt offerings because not one of them had fallen before they returned in peace." (1 Maccabees 5:54)

At the same time, Simon in Galilee was having a similar success. His army was able to overcome all the towns that resisted him and, finally, he won a great victory at the gates of Ptolemais (Acre). Then he, too, gathered together the Jews living in Galilee and brought all the families into Judea.

THE MAIN SYRIAN ARMY INVADES

Far away in the Persian province of his empire, the Seleucid king Antiochus Epiphanes died. His heir was the young Antiochus V, called Eupator. His guardian was General Lysias who, for the moment, controlled the whole empire although his position was threatened by a rival general Phillipos.

Bringing the young king with him, Lysias set out (163-2 B.C.E.) to make a final end of these irritating Jews who, under their rebel leader, were now attempting to liquidate the Syrian garrison of the Akra in Jerusalem. This time, Lysias came not as the governor of a province, with a local inefficient force. He was at the head of the great national

Syrian army, with its rows of well-trained foot soldiers, its cavalry, its siege equipment and its war elephants.

War elephants were the tanks of the ancient world. Heavily armoured, with a wooden cage raised above it, each elephant formed a moving tower for 3 archers who stood on its back, while

The tanks of the ancient world. War elephant from the 3rd century B.C.E.

around it, on each side and behind, came anything up to a thousand foot soldiers and 500 horsemen. On this campaign, Lysias had 32 such formidable weapons, in addition — if we were to believe literally the author of the First book of Maccabees — to 100,000 infantry and 20,000 cavalry. These figures are certainly exaggerated. But whatever the actual size of the force, it was too much for Judas and his little band.

Lysias first of all attacked the Maccabean fortress of Beth-Zur, south of Jerusalem, bringing up battering rams and "siege engines" to break into its walls and making "mounds to shoot from"

Maccabean wall of the fortress of Beth-Zur. The lower wall protected the base of the stronger, inner wall.

Reconstruction of a Roman battering ram. A team of soldiers hauled on the ropes to pull it back. When they let go, the ram was hurled against the wall to "batter" it down.

(towers as high as the walls from which archers could shoot onto the heads of the defenders).

The place was captured and a Syrian garrison left in control. Then Lysias turned to his major battle with Judas at Beth-Zechariah :

> "And the king got up early in the morning and moved his army precipitately along the road to Beth-Zechariah, and his forces armed themselves for battle, and sounded the trumpets. And they showed the elephants the juice of grapes and mulberries to incite them to battle." (1 Maccabees 6:33-34)

The whole army made an impressive sight :

> "And when the sun fell on the gold and brass shields, the mountains flashed back and shone like blazing torches... And all who

Judas and his men faced this terrifying horde
and gave a good account of themselves. His brother
Eleazar looking at one of the approaching columns
saw that its central elephant had the royal arms on
its breastplates. This must be the king's own elephant! If he could kill it he would be destroying
their arch-enemy at the same time. He grasped his
sword and charged into the ranks of foot soldiers
that surrounded it, killing right and left until he
came right up to the great beast. He crept under
the elephant and, with a mighty thrust of his sword,
slit open its belly. The elephant staggered, died and
fell, the great wooden tower on its back falling
among the soldiers, the archers jumping for their
lives. But Eleazar was too close to run. He was
caught under the falling body and crushed to death.

His was only one example of the heroism of the
Jewish soldiers, but the strength of Lysias was too
great. Though "six hundred of the king's men" fell
that day, Judas had to beat a retreat and leave the
way to Jerusalem open to Lysias.

For a moment Judas was in despair. But, to
Lysias, the war in Judea was a secondary affair.
His victory was never followed up. News came to
him that Phillipos was marching on Antioch from
eastern Syria. Lysias hastily concluded a peace
with Judas so that he could be free to return home
to Antioch and deal with affairs there.

The first objective of the Maccabees had been gained. As a condition of the peace, Antiochus' Decrees against the Jewish religion were officially annulled. In a proclamation from King Antiochus Eupator to his general Lysias, the king wrote :

"King Antiochus sends greeting to his brother Lysias. Now that our father has departed to the gods, we desire the subjects of the kingdom to be unmolested and to busy themselves with the care of their own affairs, and as we have heard that the Jews will not agree to our father's policy of making them adopt Greek practices, but prefer their own way of living, and ask to be allowed to follow their own customs, we wish this nation also to be undisturbed and our decision is that their temple be returned to them, and that they follow their ancestral customs." (2 Maccabees 11:22-25)

Judas' conquest of Jerusalem and the rededication of the Temple had in fact restored religious freedom. Now, legal recognition was given to a return to the situation that had existed before Antiochus had decreed the persecution. The Temple was to be used only by Jews. Syrians were in future forbidden to interfere or to practise their pagan cults there. Although Judea remained a part of the Seleucid empire, Jerusalem was again the capital of a more-or-less self-governing Jewish province. The hellenistic reform aimed against the ancient traditions, was abolished.

But this was to be only a breathing space. Power in Judea clearly rested in the hands of Judas and his followers, but a Greek garrison remained in occupation of the Akra in Jerusalem, acting as a last stronghold of the hellenizers. The Syrians felt that they had been let down. Lysias revenged himself on the one who had suggested military intervention in Judea — Menelaus. The erstwhile High Priest of Israel was dragged from his prison in Antioch and brutally executed by being roasted to death in a slow fire on the sacrificial altar.

However, someone to take his place had to be found. It must be someone who would please the masses of the people without too openly affronting the hellenists — whose wealth and position still made them a force in the state. To the Syrians, of course, Judas was little more than a successful brigand chief. He was passed over and the choice fell on Eliakim (who, fashionably, spelt his name Greek fashion, Alcimus). He seems to have belonged to the Onias family, traditionally high priests, which means that he was a member of the upper, hellenizing class. Such a man as High Priest was too much for Judas to swallow. He refused to accept him. Rejected, Alcimus returned to Antioch and appealed for support.

RENEWED HELLENIZATION

He found that there had been another change of ruler. Antiochus and Lysias had been murdered and the throne taken by Demetrius, (the son of Seleucus Philopator), the rightful heir to the throne. He hoped to placate the Jews by putting their traditional religious leader at their head and sent Alcimus back to Judea, supported by an army under the Syrian Governor, Bacchides.

The plan was successful with at least one section of the rebels. The Hassidim warrior-priests who had been the backbone of Judas' army when it was fighting a holy war for religion, were content to have achieved the annullment of the Decrees. They accepted the new leader for, they said, "A priest of the blood of Aron has come with the forces and he will not do us any wrong." (1 Maccabees 7:14).

The Hassidim were, very largely, the learned scribes. They wanted Alcimus to accept them as official interpreters of "the ancestral laws" which covered so much more than questions of pure religion. In fact, they were claiming the right to a say in all the details of running the country.

Alcimus was a hellenizer. While he was High Priest, the movement towards hellenization continued, just as in earlier generations. Negotiations between him and the Hassidim were doomed from the start. Finally he had sixty of them arrested and killed "in a single day". The survivors returned to Judas' camp where, after a three year truce, the civil war was taken up again.

Bacchides had gone back to Antioch, leaving Alcimus in charge. The people of Jerusalem were solidly on the side of Judas. With clashes between the two sides occurring daily in the streets, the High Priest put the governing of Judea into the hands of a Syrian officer and hastened back to Antioch with a fresh appeal for military support.

JUDAS CONFRONTS NICANOR

The king sent a large army, led by Nicanor, "one of his distinguished officers, who hated Israel bitterly", with orders to destroy nationalist Jewry. Nicanor began with a deceitfully friendly message to Judas, saying,

> "Let us have no battle between me and you. I will come with a few men to have a peaceable personal meeting." (1 Mac. 7: 28)

The two leaders met and Nicanor discovered Judas to be a responsible man of affairs and an attractive companion. Relations between them became so amicable that Judas even followed the Syrian leader's advice to "marry, settle down and take his part in life."

However, news of this state of affairs was gall to the official High Priest Alcimus, still waiting in Antioch. He hurried to the king with complaints of Nicanor's disobedience — he said treachery. As a result, Demetrius sent an order to Nicanor demanding that Judas be sent post-haste to Antioch — in chains.

To find himself out of favour with his king put Nicanor in a very bad temper. While he was looking for an opportunity to carry out the king's order, Judas, finding himself suddenly treated very coldly, gathered his supporters and went into hiding, away from Jerusalem. This was a serious blow to Nica-

Warfare and weapons were unchanged two centuries after Alexander defeated the Persians at Issus (detail from jacket).

A valuable ring was a fitting present from a Seleucid king to his friend (see p. 29).

Threshing floor amid the olive groves of the hills of Galilee, a scene that has altered little since the time of the Hasmoneans.

nor's plans. He stormed down to the Temple, at the time of sacrifice and demanded Judas' whereabouts from the assembled priests. They did not know where he was, but Nicanor vowed :

"If you do not hand Judas over to me as a prisoner, I will level this sacred precinct of God with the ground and tread down the altar, and build here a splendid temple to Dionysus." (2 Mac. 15:13)

VENGEANCE AT BETH-HORON

Such a threat was a clear warning of renewed Syrian oppression. Nicanor assembled his forces, some nine thousand well equipped and trained soldiers, and marched out of Jerusalem westwards towards Beth-horon, where he hoped to meet a second great army sent him from Syria. The road winds down from Jerusalem through a rocky pass and there, above him, on the heights of Adasa, Judas and his 3,000 men waited in ambush.

"Nicanor and his men advanced with trumpets and battle songs. And Judas and his men met the enemy with entreaties and prayers. So fighting with their hands and praying to God with their hearts, they laid low no less than thirty-five thousand, being greatly cheered by God's manifest aid." (2 Maccabees 15: 26-27)

(By the time the oft-told story was related by the author of Second Maccabees the number of the Syrians had grown somewhat !). The victory itself, however, was no exaggeration. The routed Syrians were chased as far as Gezer, 35 kilometres distant and the way was littered with their dead.

Among the dead, lay Nicanor himself. As a fitting punishment for his threats against their holy

The heights and pass of Beth-horon, midway between Jerusalem and the coast. Here Judas won his great victory over Nicanor.

city, the Jewish force cut off his head and arm and sent them to Jerusalem where they were displayed as a warning. To celebrate their victory, Judas proclaimed a "feast of the day of Nicanor", which was celebrated regularly for a few years. Their enemy lay dead and the Jews could hope for peace for a little longer.

THE ROMAN SENATE WELCOMES THE JEWS

In fact Judas knew that, facing the whole might of the Syrian empire, he was in a very dangerous position. For help, he turned to Syria's rivals — Rome. Messengers from the Maccabees appeared before the Roman Senate and said,

"Judas, who is called Maccabeus, and his brothers and the Jewish people have sent us to you, to make an alliance and firm peace with you and that we may be enrolled as allies and friends of yours." (1 Maccabees 2: 20)

The Roman Senate was pleased with this proposal. The Jews had the reputation of being good and brave soldiers and, in any case, Rome natural-

Sailing galley from the mosaic in the Street of the Corporations, business center for Rome's port of Ostia. Ships like this sailed out of Ostia to all the ports of the Mediterranean, including far-off Joppa, their travellers entertained by the gambolling dolphins.

ly encouraged any enemies of their Syrian rivals. Their answer, "inscribed on tablets of brass", offered the Jews a mutual defence pact and promised them support (which was never given) in their quarrel with the Syrian king. But the journey to Rome was a long and dangerous one in those days. It was two years before the messengers returned and by then, the reply brought no comfort to Judas.

JUDAS' LAST BATTLE

The news of Nicanor's death and defeat made the Syrian king angrier than ever with the Jews. In the spring of the next year, he sent Alcimus and general Bacchides back to Palestine at the head of a great army of twenty thousand men and two thousand horse. They first destroyed the stronghold of Arbel, west of the Sea of Galilee, and then threatened Jerusalem.

Judas' army was no larger than 2,000 men but, with these, he hoped to be able to repeat the tactics that had proved successful before, and launch a surprise attack. But he was unlucky. This time the enemy was expecting him. His force reached the heights of Elasa to see the whole Syrian might arrayed against them. The sight was too much for many of the Jewish soldiers and when Judas called the roll of his troops, he found he had eight hundred men with which to fight against the Syrians. Desperately he tried to rally them, but his men were afraid. It would be better, they suggested, to come back another day with a full force. But Judas cried,

"I will never do this thing, and flee from them; and if our time has come, let us die bravely for our brothers, and not leave a stain upon our honour." (1 Maccabees 9: 10)

The Syrians were drawn up in two wings and, with all his old courage, Judas attacked the right wing, commanded by Bacchides, and drove it into the mountains. Encouraged, his men raced in pursuit. But they were too few. The other wing of the Syrians came after them and attacked from behind. The Jews were caught between the two armies. Bravely though they fought, it was hopeless. When Judas fell dead among so many of his companions, the few that were left fled.

The battle and, it seemed, the whole liberation struggle were lost. Five years earlier, Judas had first rallied his countrymen to stand against those who were oppressing them. Now, his brothers sadly took up his body and buried him in the tombs of his forefathers in Modiin.

"And they wept over him, and all Israel lamented him greatly and mourned for a long time, saying, 'What a hero is fallen, the Saviour of Israel!'" (1 Maccabees 9: 20-21)

Arrowheads from the Maccabean wars.

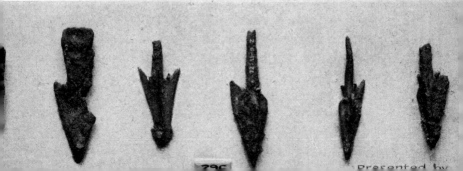

Chapter V

THE HASMONEAN PERIOD

JONATHAN RALLIES THE DEFEATED

The nation mourned its dead leader. Bacchides and the hellenizers, it seemed, had triumphed. For the next two years they remained in control of the country and the situation of the Maccabeans seemed desperate. Returning partisans and all who were known to have favoured the Maccabean cause were terrorized by the new government and many were imprisoned in the Jerusalem Akra fortress. Because of the years of fighting, many farms had been left neglected and even "the very ground appeared to rebel" against the Jews and there was famine in the land.

Nevertheless, neither Syrian power nor the terror of Alcimus and his party could bring peace to the land. Even though their leader was dead, there were still those who believed that the Hasmonean family were to be preferred to Syrian rulers and their henchmen. They turned to Judas' younger brother, Jonathan, nicknamed Apphus or "the wary" and asked him to be their leader.

"I am ready to die for you" answered Jonathan and he became their general.

He organized small guerrilla bands which went through the country harrassing Bacchides and his men. Bacchides marched out with his whole army against Jonathan but, in the marshes that lined the Jordan, Jonathan gave him the slip. For the time being he knew that he must accept the position of an outlaw leader and he established his headquarters with his family and a number of supporters, including Hassidim, at Tekoa, in the wilderness east of Jerusalem. While they were there, the eldest Hasmonean brother, Johanan was murdered by a tribe of Arabs.

Guerrilla warfare continued. As a defence, Bacchides built a string of forts encircling the country, which could, if necessary, act as a last refuge for the hellenizers' party. Confident that he had thus done everything he could for the hellenizers, he returned to more pressing affairs in Antioch, leaving Alicimus, as he thought, in control of the situation.

SLOW RECOVERY

For two long years Jonathan waited. Much less impulsive than his brother, he was content to keep the hellenizers too uneasy for excesses against the Jews while at the same time he avoided annoying Antioch by any notable victories.

However, at the end of that time the situation was changed. In Jerusalem Alcimus died and the hellenists laid a plot to capture and kill Jonathan and all the surviving members of the Hasmonean family. Surely by such an action, the rebellion would finally be destroyed. The plotters counted without Jonathan's intelligence service. Instead of the Hasmonean leaders, the ones who died were fifty Syrian and hellenist officials involved in the plot. At last Jonathan had triumphed, but his action brought Bacchides back at the head of a new army. Once again he was defeated. Jonathan and Simon had made themselves a stronghold at Bethbasi. Bacchides laid siege to it but, one night, the two brothers led their armies secretly out of the fortress. They made two separate surprise attacks on the Syrian camp, and destroyed it.

In a furious rage, Bacchides returned to Jerusalem and avenged himself on many of the hellenizers there who had so rashly advised him to come into their country again. Bacchides had seen how little real power or influence they had. The authority in the country, he realized, was Jonathan and his party. Apart from a tiny section of the aristocracy and wealthy men, the people had come to accept the leadership of the Hasmoneans.

AN HONOURABLE PEACE

Accordingly, he made peace with Jonathan. No formal treaty was drawn up, but prisoners were exchanged and Bacchides swore "that he would not seek to injure him as long as he lived."

Jonathan set up a government at Michmash, an old township a little distance north-east of Jerusalem, at the place where, 900 years before, another Jonathan, the son of King Saul, had won his victory over the Philistines. There, the Maccabean Jonathan "judged Israel" as of old.

Ten years had passed since the rebellion had begun under Judas. As a result of the Maccabean War
of Liberation, the Decrees of Antiochus had been
annulled; the Jewish religion had been rescued and
revived and a successful war of revenge had been
waged against the gentile inhabitants of Palestine.

The hellenists had always needed Syrian aid, for
they fought in isolation with Syrian help to support them. Judas as the strong personality at the
core of the Jewish rebellion and his comrades, on
the other hand, had the open sympathy and help
of the people of the whole countryside. In the end,
this had been recognized by the Syrians and the
royally approved government of Judea was in the
hands of the popular, no-longer rebel leader, Jonathan the Hasmonean. In future, when the Syrian
government wanted the support of the people of
Judea, they would use diplomatic negotiation, not
force. Judas did not live to see this, but he had
shown his people the way towards independence.

THE SELEUCID EMPIRE IN DECLINE

The story of Jonathan and the Jews for the next
ten years is one of military successes and growing
power. Jewish progress was closely bound up with
the slow decline of the Seleucid dynasty.

Their empire had long passed its peak and whole
provinces, like Parthia, Bactria and others in central Asia, had already achieved independence. In
order to keep together as much as was left to him,
the Syrian king granted self-government to the

provinces of his empire who acknowledged him as king. Palestine under Jonathan could fit into such an organization as an equal partner.

Against the background of slow decay externally, the Seleucid court at Antioch became the scene of constant intrigues and rivalries. One group in opposition to the rightful king Demetrius set up a usurper, Alexander Balas, as a rival monarch, with his capital in Ptolemais (Acre). Both he and Demetrius began to look around for supporters. Most important was the ruler of neighbouring Judea.

JONATHAN ACKNOWLEDGED BY THE ENEMY

The aristocracy, the party of the hellenizers, were powerless in the country and had not even had a High Priest for seven years. The only important personality in the country, with enough energy and military experience to be of any use, was Jonathan. Demetrius was the first to understand this. Trying to forestall Alexander Balas, he formally acknowledged Jonathan's position, offered him an alliance, gave him permission to raise troops and released the Jewish hostages who had been held prisoner in the Akra ever since their capture by Bacchides.

Jonathan moved to Jerusalem and, with the authority of Demetrius, as military leader of Judea, installed himself and his government in the ancient capital. The hellenizers were put to flight and the city fortified. Greek garrisons were expelled from the country, with the exception of the soldiers in the Akra and in the fortress of Beth-zur, which became a refuge for the fleeing hellenizers.

JONATHAN THE FIRST HASMONEAN HIGH PRIEST

Alexander Balas and Demetrius drew up their armies and began to battle for the throne. At first Demetrius was successful and Alexander in his turn looked around for help. In order to win over the Jews to his side, he wrote to his "brother" Jonathan, naming him a "Friend" and appointing him High Priest. With the letter went a purple robe and a crown of gold. At the Feast of Tabernacles (October 152 B.C.E.), Jonathan officiated for the first time as High Priest.

This set the seal on the victory of the Hasmoneans. The civil war was over; the hellenistic Jews finally silenced. For the first time since biblical days, a Jewish ruler in Palestine, commanding his own army, was a leading figure in the Near Eastern world. This had been the dream of the Tobiads and the hellenizers. But how differently it had come true ! The land of Judea was a force in international politics, not as a hellenistic vassal of Syria, but as a semi-independent Jewish state controlled by its own Jewish leaders. A sound foundation had been laid for the future Hasmonean dynasty.

JONATHAN HONOURED BY SYRIA

For the moment Judea remained part of the Seleucid empire, or confederation. Demetrius tried to win Jonathan back to his side, but that "wily" ruler ignored all the future benefits that were suddenly held out to him. Alexander Balas was a favourite in Rome and Jonathan knew better than to do anything to annoy that increasingly powerful factor in world politics.

His judgment was soon proved sound. Demetrius died in battle and Alexander, now enthroned unopposed in Antioch, appointed Jonathan "Strategos" and "meridarch", military and civil governor of Judea. This additional appointment made Jonathan, as High Priest, a high royal official of the Seleucid empire and sole ruler of all aspects of his country's life. Another milestone on the road to full independence had been passed !

A CHALLENGE FROM ALEXANDER'S RIVAL

Jonathan's loyalty to Alexander was tested five years later when a new Demetrius, son of the defeated king, appeared to claim the throne that was rightfully his. Alexander had appointed another Apollonius as governor of Coele-Syria, but no sooner had he established garrisons in Joppa and Jamnia in the coastal plain, traditionally hostile to the Jews, than he declared in support of Demetrius and sent a challenge to Jonathan, as Alexander's ally :

"Why do you claim your authority against us up in the mountains? If you really trust in your troops come down into the plain to us and let us measure our strength together there, for I have control of the towns... your forefathers have been routed twice in their land. So now you will not be able to stand against the cavalry and such a force as this on the plain, where there is no stone or pebble, or place to escape to." (1 Maccabees 10: 70-73)

In fact, his jibe was well founded. The Hasmoneans had never had any success against cavalry, chariots or without the help of mountainous country. Nevertheless, Jonathan was not going to let such a taunt go unanswered.

At the head of an army of 10,000 men he marched down to the coast and took possession of Joppa, thereby cutting off Apollonius' line of retreat to Antioch in the north. The Syrian army, eight thousand foot-soldiers and three thousand horsemen, left its camp at Jamnia and retreated southwards towards Ashdod tempting the Jewish army further along the coast. This exposed them to a sudden attack in the rear from a thousand horsemen Apollonius had stationed as an ambush. All day long the cavalry charged the Jewish columns, showering them with arrows, and all day long the Jews stood firm. The ground was soft and by the end of the day the horses were worn out. At this, Simon and a second wing of the Jewish army advanced to the rescue, scattering the exhausted Syrian cavalry and driving the foot soldiers before them into Ashdod. There, they took refuge in the temple of Dagon, their pagan idol. He was no help to them, however. Jonathan pursued the fleeing Syrians into Ashdod, burned the temple to the ground and destroyed and plundered the town.

Greek archer. This classic carving of the 6th century B.C.E. stood above the entrance to the Temple of Ergine in Greece.

As a result of the battle, the town of Askalon immediately surrendered to Jonathan, and the last Syrian strongholds in the southern plain were destroyed. In addition, as a reward, Alexander Balas awarded Jonathan the town and district of Ekron. The Jews thus established a foothold within the Philistine coastline, giving the country an outlet to the Mediterranean with all the possibilities for development and prosperity that that carried with it. The capture of Joppa, indeed was the beginning of a great expansion in Jewish trade, just as the absorption of the other independent cities strengthened the whole economy of the growing Hasmonean state.

Greek horseman.

Jonathan's position seemed secure in every way. His country thrived. Its trade grew. He even managed to keep on good terms with both sides in the Seleucid dynastic struggle. When, eight years later, Alexander Balas was murdered and Demetrius took his place, Jonathan presented himself before the new young king, splendidly robed as High Priest, attended by an impressive escort of priests and elders, and bearing tempting gifts in gold, silver, precious stuffs and jewels.

Demetrius was enchanted. He confirmed all the offices and dignities of the High Priest, inscribed Jonathan in the list of his very "first Friends" and added the frontier districts of Ephraim, Lod, and Ramathaim (from the province of Samaria) to the realm of Judea. Moreover, in return for the substantial bribe of 300 talents, Demetrius exempted all observing Jews from the taxes on grain and fruit they had previously paid. This privilege was extended to the newly acquired districts, a good way of increasing Hasmonean popularity among the many Jews who lived there!

JEWISH TROOPS IN ANTIOCH RESCUE DEMETRIUS

In all Judea, the only remaining evidence of Seleucid domination was the little refuge of the hellenists in the Akra fortress, still garrisoned by Syrian soldiers. Jonathan had long wanted to get rid of this thorn in his side and thought he had found an opportunity when troubles started again for Demetrius in Antioch. The king appealed for help to his "Friend" and Jonathan sent him 3,000 soldiers against a vague promise to withdraw the Akra garrison. The promise was never kept but the Jewish soldiers proved their value in Antioch when a mob gathered — a hundred and twenty thousand strong according to the First book of Maccabees — and attacked the palace, meaning to kill him. Only Jonathan's soldiers were any help to the distraught king. They were able to restore order and, for the moment, save the king and his throne.

Demetrius thanked his Jewish helpers and sent them home. But he found a strange way to show his gratitude. Another letter went to Jonathan revoking the tax privilege recently granted and threatening a new war against the Jews.

A NEW ANTIOCHUS WOOS JONATHAN'S FRIENDSHIP

Demetrius began to prepare for the attack. But before he was ready, he was faced with a new enemy at home. Alexander Balas had left a son. While the boy was still a child, one of his father's generals, Tryphon, decided to use the unstable situation to make him king. He, Tryphon, would be of course, the real power behind the throne. With the boy at his side and a powerful army behind him, Tryphon was able to drive Demetrius away. A new young Antiochus sat on the throne in Antioch. But Demetrius remained in control of much of the country. To get his hands on Coele-Syria, Tryphon needed the help of the Jews. He sent presents to Jonathan, confirmed him as High Priest, and granted him the valuable right to wear purple and drink from a cup of gold ! More substantially, he added a further district to the northern frontier of Judea. To Simon, who acted as Jonathan's commander-in-chief, Tryphon, in the name of Antiochus, promised the governorship of the whole coastline of Western Palestine, "from the ladder of Tyre unto the borders of Egypt", with Ptolemais (Acre) as his base.

Thus both the Hasmonean princes became high officials of the Seleucid state, with a good deal of independent authority and this they put to good use. In support of Antiochus, Jonathan campaigned east of Jordan as far north as Damascus over country that, twenty years earlier, had seen his

Gold and silver dishes and cups found in Pompei. Tableware like this was used not only by Greeks and Romans but also in homes of Jewish princes.

Entrance to the Hasmonean castle of Gezer, an important town in the lowlands of Judea.

brother's campaigns as a struggling rebel leader. Now, Jonathan used his royal authority to free Judea of the last Syrian strongholds and to strengthen Jewish power. Simon set out to capture the Syrian garrison at Beth-Zur and man it with Jewish troops. Then he made sorties against the hellenistic ports, Askalon and Joppa. Although the brothers may have described their activities as in the interests of the Syrian king, they were in fact carefully strengthening the foundations of an independent Judea. By the end of their campaigns, Hasmonean rule over Judea was almost complete. The country's defences were strengthened and, to protect the capital from attack, Jonathan built a wall right around the Akra in Jerusalem intending to starve its garrison out.

The position of the Hasmoneans seemed assured. While Jonathan was strengthening the fortifications of Judea, he was at the same time using diplomacy to maintain the country's position abroad.

First of all he sent a delegation to Rome to confirm the alliance which Judas had made. He also made approaches to the Spartans in Greece asking them to renew the friendly relations established years earlier when Onias was High Priest of Israel. At that time, following the custom of the times, the Spartan king had written of the brotherhood that should exist between the two peoples because both, he claimed, were descended from Abraham. Arius, king of the Spartans, had written :

> "It has been found in a writing concerning the Spartans and Jews, that they are kinsmen, and that they are descended from Abraham. Now since we have learned this, please write us about your welfare. We for our part write you that your cattle and property are ours and ours are yours." (1 Maccabees 12: 21-23)

Talk of ancestors shared by Jew and Spartan might be a polite fiction. It is however a good indication of the high international standing of the Hasmoneans and the people they led.

Jonathan had his eye to the future. Even if his Roman alliance had never been of practical use to Judas, its renewal must have increased Hasmonean prestige with the peoples of Greece and the Orient.

Jonathan had good reason to feel warmly towards Antiochus, the young boy who was his sovereign. His affection was well-known and when Tryphon, tired of acting merely as a second-in-command, aimed at taking over the throne for himself, he knew he must first get rid of Antiochus' powerful Jewish ally.

Supported by a large army, Tryphon marched into Galilee, where Jonathan met him, seemingly as an ally, at Beth-shean, at the head of "forty thousand picked fighting men." This was more than Tryphon had bargained for.

Jonathan had the reputation of being a wily man, but Tryphon beat him at his own game. Instead of the arrest he had planned, he treated Jonathan with all respect. "Why have you burdened all these people, when there is no war between us ?" asked Tryphon. He had only come into Judea for the purpose of making Jonathan a present of the town of Ptolemais (Acre) and, for this, there was no need of such a great army. Additional honours seemed natural to Jonathan now and he believed Tryphon. Dismissing all but three thousand of his men he and a small troop of one thousand men marched confidently into Ptolemais, banners waving, expecting a triumphant welcome.

But no sooner had they all entered the city, than the gates were closed behind them. Jonathan was taken prisoner and had to watch, helpless, as his soldiers were massacred. Too late, he could judge how far Tryphon was to be trusted !

The two thousand soldiers who were awaiting him in the plain were chased back into the hills of Judea where they brought the shattering news of Jonathan's fate and the sudden enmity of Tryphon. Without a leader, with no friend on either side of the Seleucid realm, the Jews realized that a wave of hellenistic domination was likely to renew all the persecutions they had believed at an end. Once again, the whole future of Jewry seemed threatened. No wonder the people wept for their lost leader:

"And all Israel mourned for him bitterly. And all the heathen around them tried to destroy them utterly, for they said, 'They have no leader or helper, so now let us make war on them and destroy their memory from among men.'" (1 Maccabees 12: 53)

Chapter VI

FULL INDEPENDENCE

"THE YOKE OF THE HEATHEN LIFTED FROM ISRAEL"

SIMON TAKES HIS BROTHERS' PLACE

Once again from the depths of despair, the Hasmoneans were to snatch victory. The last of the sons of Mattathias, Simon, now stepped forward to the leadership of his despondent people.

He encouraged them — and led them to new deeds of liberation. First of all the defences of Jerusalem were strengthened. Then an army took control of the port of Joppa, drove away its gentile inhabitants and settled the town with Jews. The harbour was secured for Jewish trade and Tryphon's route along the coast was blocked. For Tryphon was advancing to the attack with a large army — and Jonathan, his prisoner, in chains.

A message came to Simon from Tryphon :

> "...send a hundred talents of silver and two of his (Jonathan's) sons as hostages so that when he is released he will not revolt against us, and we will let him go." (1 Maccabees 13:16)

But, of course, he did not. Even when the money and the children were sent, against Simon's better judgment, Tryphon continued to advance with Jonathan still an unwilling member of the expedition.

The army reached the historic pass of Bethhoron to find it closely guarded by Simon and his

army in the fortress of Adida. Tryphon pressed south, hoping to reach Jerusalem by a roundabout route through uninhabited country east of the Jordan. But it was winter as he approached his destination. In the high Hebron hills, snow fell heavily all one night and Tryphon's cavalry found their horses shivering and slithering helplessly. Unable to go forward, Tryphon had to sound the retreat and his army made for home by the easier route to Coele-Syria.

DEATH OF JONATHAN

But he had not finished with the Hasmoneans. Once safely on their own territory, Tryphon's army

Rock tombs of Modiin where the Maccabeans were buried. The heavy stones in the picture to the left covered the entrances to the tombs which were hewn out of the rock. Burials were made in niches cut out of the sides of connecting chambers (H, G and F above).

made a single sally into the country of Gilead, east of Jordan, and here Jonathan was put to death. The once-powerful Hasmonean prince who had brought his country so far on its road to independence, died alone, apparently abandoned by his family and friends.

But, as soon as the Syrian army was cleared out, Simon sent for his brother's body and took it to Modiin. There, by the side of his father and brothers and his forefathers, Jonathan was laid to rest. Over the graves Simon had a wonderful monument built and for years the greatness of Jonathan could be read in the decoration of his memorial.

Simon was left in control of a country which was still, nominally, subject to the Seleucid Empire. The Jews still paid a yearly tribute to the king in Antioch and a Syrian garrison still controlled the Akra fortress in Jerusalem.

But the empire was doomed. Popular opposition to Tryphon, who had had the boy-king murdered and had taken his title for himself, brought the exiled Demetrius back for a warm welcome from his subjects.

Simon sent offers of help and, in return for Jewish soldiers, Demetrius confirmed Simon as High Priest and gave Judah exemption from all taxes.

This was almost equivalent to granting them independence. A city was "free" if she paid no tribute. Now, therefore, in the year 142 B.C.E., the Jews could at last think of themselves again as a free and independent people:

> "... the yoke of the heathen was lifted from Israel. And the people began to write in their contracts and agreements, 'In the first year of Simon, the great high priest and governor and commander of the Jews." (1 Maccabees 13:42)

When, in the next year, the Jews finally took possession of the Akra and expelled the last foreign soldiers from their capital, the victory was complete. Without Syrian support, the hellenizers were helpless. Now their party was utterly crushed and the Jews could look forward to years of tranquility.

Charter guaranteeing freedom to the city of Tasos by the second century B.C.E. king of Commagene in Asia Minor. This record of its right to self-government was typical of hellenistic cities.

Quarter silver shekels struck by the Jews after their independence had been gained under Simon, the founder of the Hasmonean dynasty.

The shofar, or ram's horn. This was sounded on High Holidays, and other important occasions.

A year later, "a great congregation of priests and people and leaders of the nation and elders of the country" gathered together to set up a constitution for their Jewish state. Simon was proclaimed High Priest and military and civil governor of the Jews. The office was made hereditary, which meant that the people agreed to be ruled by a Hasmonean prince for ever. The Hasmonean dynasty was established.

Whatever troubles and disasters lay in store for the Jewish people, Simon knew, as he heard the proclamation read, that the great Liberation struggle which he and his brothers had begun had finally been successful. The Jewish religion had been saved. The Jews' great contribution of the idea of a single universal God was to become part of the future of civilization. A free, independent Jewry, under its own national leaders, could face the world as an equal. Shortly after, Judea would be ruled by Hasmonean Kings. The aims for which Judas Maccabaeus, his brothers, and so many of his people had died, had been realized. What had begun as a wild dream of impossible glory had been transformed into a glittering reality.

No wonder the chronicler of Simon's reign could say :

> "He made peace in the land, and Israel rejoiced with great joy. Each man sat under his vine and his fig tree, and there was no one that could make them afraid. ... In his days matters prospered in his hands." (1 Maccabees 14: 12,36)

ACKNOWLEDGMENTS OF ILLUSTRATIONS